THE ALLYSHIP CHALLENGE

Journal

Self-Reflection to Move Beyond Performative Allyship and Become a Genuine Accomplice

ALLYSHIP
Publishing, LLC

Copyright © 2022 Kimberly Harden

All rights reserved.

ISBN: 979-8-218-08117-1

Cover Design: Sean Bobbato

Cover Copyright © 2022 Allyship Publishing, LLC

Printed in the USA

This book or parts thereof may not be reproduced in any form, stored in a retrieval system, or transmitted in any form or by any means—electronic, mechanical, photocopying, recording, scanning—or without prior written permission of the publisher, except as provided by United States of America copyright law.

Limit of liability/Disclaimer of Warranty: While the publisher and author have used their best efforts in preparing this book, they make no representations or warranties with respect to the accuracy or completeness of the contents of this book and specifically disclaim any implied warranties of merchantability or fitness for a particular purpose. No warranty may be created or extended by sales representatives or written sales materials. The advice and strategies contained herein may not be suitable for your situation. Neither the publisher nor the author shall be liable for any loss of profit or any other commercial damages, including but not limited to special, incidental, consequential, or other damages.

This publication is not designed to provide authoritative information regarding the subject matter covered. It is sold with the understanding that the publisher is not rendering professional services. If legal, accounting, medical, psychological, or any other expert existence is required, the services of a competent professional person should be sought.

Library of Congress Cataloging-in-Publication Data: An application to register this book for cataloging has been submitted to the Library of Congress.

What is the difference between equality and equity?
Is one more important than the other?

What is the difference between prejudice and discrimination?

Have you been discriminated against? How did it make you feel?

Why do we feel the need to ask about someone's identity?

What steps can you take to learn about diversity, equity, and inclusion?

_____
_____
_____
_____
_____
_____
_____
_____
_____
_____
_____
_____
_____
_____
_____

Why do you think we were taught that racism was defeated when slavery and segregation ended?

_____
_____
_____
_____
_____
_____
_____
_____
_____
_____
_____
_____
_____
_____
_____

How can people become more comfortable with talking about race and diversity?

How can you appreciate cultures without appropriating them?

How should you respond to racism generally in society?
How should you respond to racism toward people you know?

How is your response to racism and/or discrimination different when it is coming from a family member, close friend, or a work colleague?

_____
_____
_____
_____
_____
_____
_____
_____
_____
_____
_____
_____
_____
_____
_____
_____

How can you maintain a good relationship with family and friends and still call out their hurtful behavior?

_____
_____
_____
_____
_____
_____
_____
_____
_____
_____
_____
_____
_____
_____
_____

Is your lack of diverse friendships due to your upbringing, location, or other circumstances? Explain your answer.

How can you develop true, authentic relationships without tokenizing?

Describe a time you engaged in bystander intervention. What happened? How did you feel?

How can you teach and encourage others about race, racism, diversity, inclusion, and equity without overstepping?

What have you done to prove you are an ally to people of color?

_____
_____
_____
_____
_____
_____
_____
_____
_____
_____
_____
_____
_____
_____
_____

How often do you move aside or say "excuse me" in order to make space for others?

How connected are you to those who are different from you? How can you develop, strengthen, and deepen that bond?

How do you show love to your immediate community? How can you expand or replicate that love outside of your community?

In what ways and how often do you edit or filter yourself so you are seen as "good"?

In what ways have you been taught that to receive better treatment you must behave differently?

What does radical activism look like to you?

What false narratives or stereotypes about yourself should you be challenging? What stories about people different from you should you be challenging?

What is total liberation?

Describe the moment when you realized that race does not determine a person's behavior or character.

Describe a time you confused invisibility with insignificance.

How often do you feel seen? How often do you see others, particularly those who have a different identity than you do?

_____

_____

_____

_____

_____

_____

_____

_____

_____

_____

_____

_____

_____

_____

How can you serve your community without trying to make the community a reflection of you?

Do you tend to throw people that have physical or mental abilities different from your own into a single pot?

What is a social construct?
Why is race a social construct?

How can you encourage and support diversity?

Tell about a time you discriminated against others. How do you feel about that time? Would you do it again?

**What privileges do you have in society?
Who granted you these privileges?
Do others have these same privileges?**

What is a microaggression? What is a common microaggression you have heard? At whom was the microaggression directed?

_____
_____
_____
_____
_____
_____
_____
_____
_____
_____
_____
_____
_____
_____
_____
_____

How should one address a microaggression when it occurs?

How can you stand up for people of color and other marginalized groups in an effective and safe manner?

Think about your circle of friends. How many people from marginalized groups are included in your friend circle?

How can you make your friendship group more diverse and inclusive?

What is a "model minority"? Does such a thing exist? If so, what's an example?

How does the idea of a "model minority" cause harm?

How are you advocating not just for yourself but for others as well?

Have you ever apologized for being in a place or taking up "too much" space? If so, why did you feel the need to do so?

_____
_____
_____
_____
_____
_____
_____
_____
_____
_____
_____
_____
_____
_____
_____

How are you using your voice, gifts, talents, and resources to transform the world?

What are the unjust acts that are considered normal and are accepted at home, at school, in the workplace, and in society?

Describe a time you were ignored, silenced, treated as less than, or given less than others. How did you feel? How often have you treated others the same way?

In what ways have you felt oppressed?

Who deserves total liberation? Who doesn't? Explain your answer.

How do you feel about being a member of your race/ethnicity?

_____
_____
_____
_____
_____
_____
_____
_____
_____
_____
_____
_____
_____
_____
_____

List some stereotypes about your race/ethnicity. Do you think they are accurate?

Do you notice a tendency in yourself to assume that people of an ethnicity other than yours share particular characteristics or behaviors? If so, what are the shared characteristics?

Define love.

Define community.

What does love for your community mean to you?

"Stay strong. Love endlessly. Change lives."
– *Amy Bleuel*

What does this mean to you?

Are your friendships mostly quantitative (many shallow relationships) or qualitative (deep connection)?

_____
_____
_____
_____
_____
_____
_____
_____
_____
_____
_____
_____
_____
_____

What privileges do you have in the workplace?

What privileges do *others* have in the workplace that you do not?

How is your response to racism and/or discrimination different when it is coming from a leader or someone in a position of authority?

On a scale of 1–5, 1 being low and 5 being high, how uncomfortable are you willing to be to ensure that all people have equal rights?

What changes are you hoping to bring about that will make your community better?

How will you support corporate social justice initiatives?

What questions do you have about race, racism, diversity, and equity that you wish your parents, guardians, and/or teachers would have discussed with you when you were younger?

_____
_____
_____
_____
_____
_____
_____
_____
_____
_____
_____
_____
_____
_____
_____
_____
_____

How can you listen supportively and compassionately to those with different opinions and values than your own?

Which avoidance strategy do you usually engage in when it comes to discussing race and difference: cognitive, emotional, or behavioral?

How can your own unique identity play a role in and support diversity, equity, and inclusion efforts?

_____
_____
_____
_____
_____
_____
_____
_____
_____
_____
_____
_____
_____
_____
_____
_____

How can you encourage your loved ones, work colleagues, and organizational leaders to have explicit conversations about DEI?

How can you promote disability-related inclusion strategies?

How can you promote age-related inclusion strategies?

Do you believe it is divisive to call out systemic bias and institutional racism? Explain your answer.

How can you move beyond "tolerance"?

How can you shift your focus from a perception of race, gender, and personality to an ethic of character, competence, and contribution?

How can you, as an employee or organizational leader, mitigate systemic bias in your organization?

How can you stop taking workplace criticisms about DEI personally?

Describe a time you sacrificed your "piece of the pie" for a marginalized colleague or friend. What were the benefits and consequences of your action?

What benefits or consequences have you experienced as a result of speaking your truth?

What do you like most about your culture?

Made in the USA
Columbia, SC
14 November 2022